Erstes Bildwörterbuch
Tiere

First Picture Dictionary
Animals

Schwein
Pig

Kaninchen
Rabbit

Schmetterling
Butterfly

Fuchs
Fox

Illustriert von Anna Ivanir

www.kidkiddos.com
Copyright ©2025 by KidKiddos Books Ltd.
support@kidkiddos.com

All rights reserved. No part of this book may be reproduced in any form or by any electronic or mechanical means, including information storage and retrieval systems, without written permission from the publisher, except in the case of a reviewer, who may quote brief passages embodied in critical articles or in a review.
First edition, 2025

Library and Archives Canada Cataloguing in Publication
First Picture Dictionary - Animals (German English Bilingual edition)
ISBN: 978-1-83416-309-3 paperback
ISBN: 978-1-83416-310-9 hardcover
ISBN: 978-1-83416-308-6 eBook

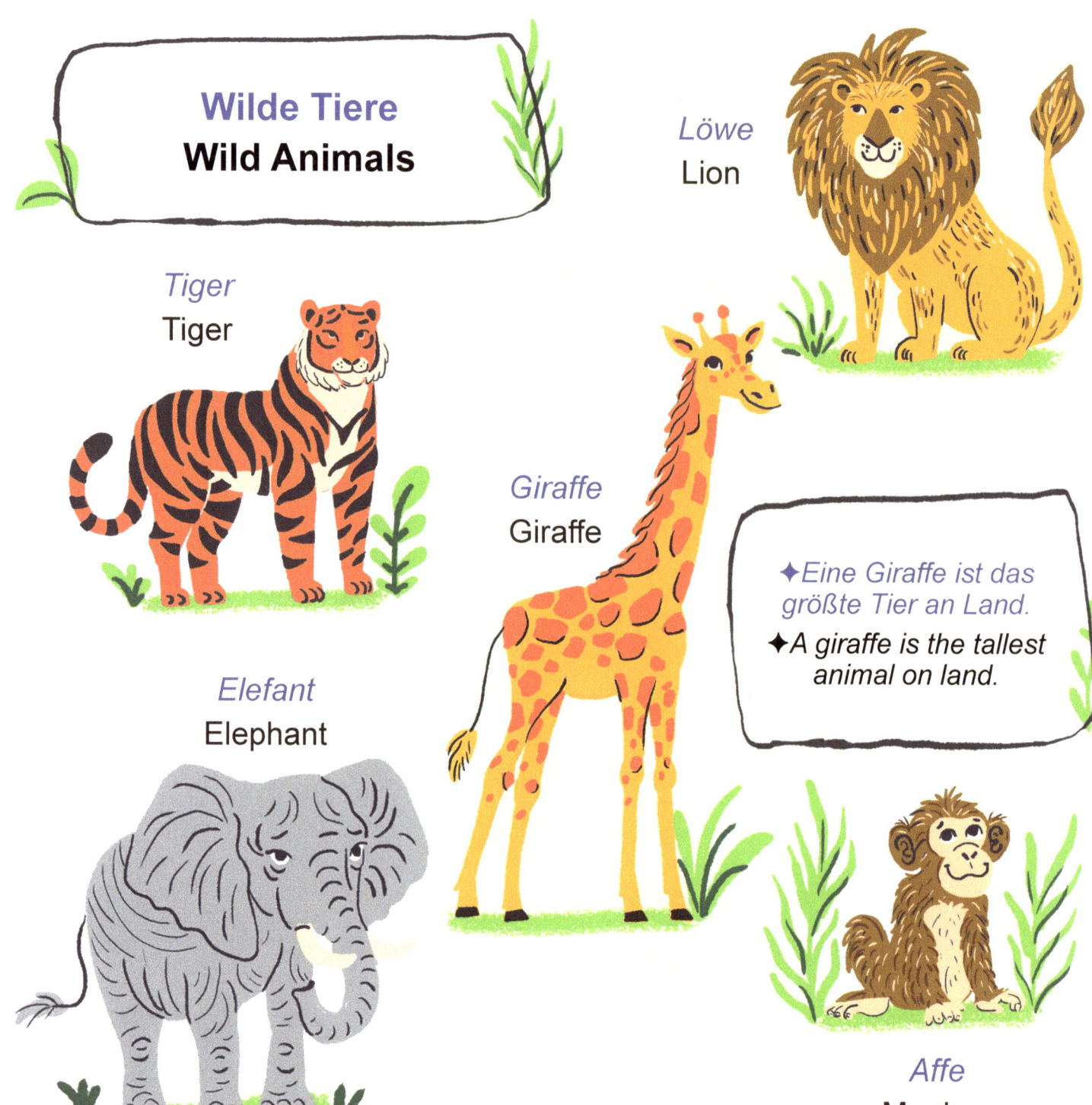

Wilde Tiere
Wild Animals

Nilpferd
Hippopotamus

Panda
Panda

Fuchs
Fox

Nashorn
Rhino

Hirsch
Deer

Elch
Moose

Wolf
Wolf

✦ *Ein Elch ist ein großartiger Schwimmer und kann unter Wasser tauchen, um Pflanzen zu fressen!*

✦ A moose is a great swimmer and can dive underwater to eat plants!

Eichhörnchen
Squirrel

Koala
Koala

✦ *Ein Eichhörnchen versteckt Nüsse für den Winter, vergisst aber manchmal, wo es sie versteckt hat!*

✦ A squirrel hides nuts for winter, but sometimes forgets where it put them!

Gorilla
Gorilla

Haustiere
Pets

Kanarienvogel
Canary

♦ *Ein Frosch kann sowohl durch die Haut als auch durch die Lunge atmen!*
♦ A frog can breathe through its skin as well as its lungs!

Meerschweinchen
Guinea Pig

Frosch
Frog

Hamster
Hamster

Goldfisch
Goldfish

Hund
Dog

✦ *Einige Papageien können Wörter nachsprechen und sogar wie ein Mensch lachen!*

✦ Some parrots can copy words and even laugh like a human!

Katze
Cat

Papagei
Parrot

Tiere auf dem Bauernhof
Animals at the Farm

Kuh
Cow

Huhn
Chicken

Ente
Duck

Schaf
Sheep

Pferd
Horse

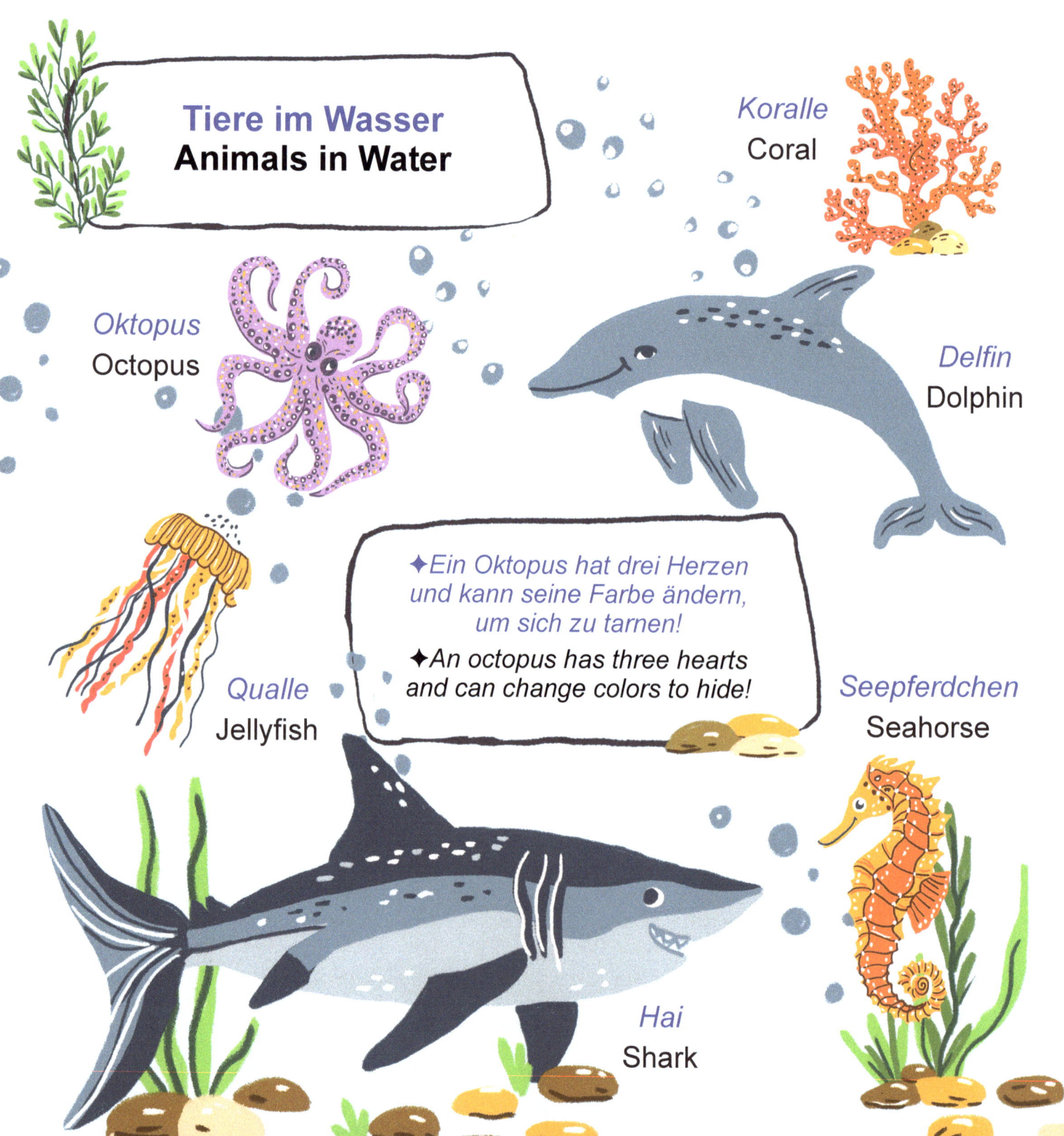

Dachs
Badger

Stachelschwein
Porcupine

Murmeltier
Groundhog

✦ *Eine Eidechse kann einen neuen Schwanz wachsen lassen, wenn sie einen verliert!*
✦ A lizard can grow a new tail if it loses one!

Eidechse
Lizard

Ameise
Ant

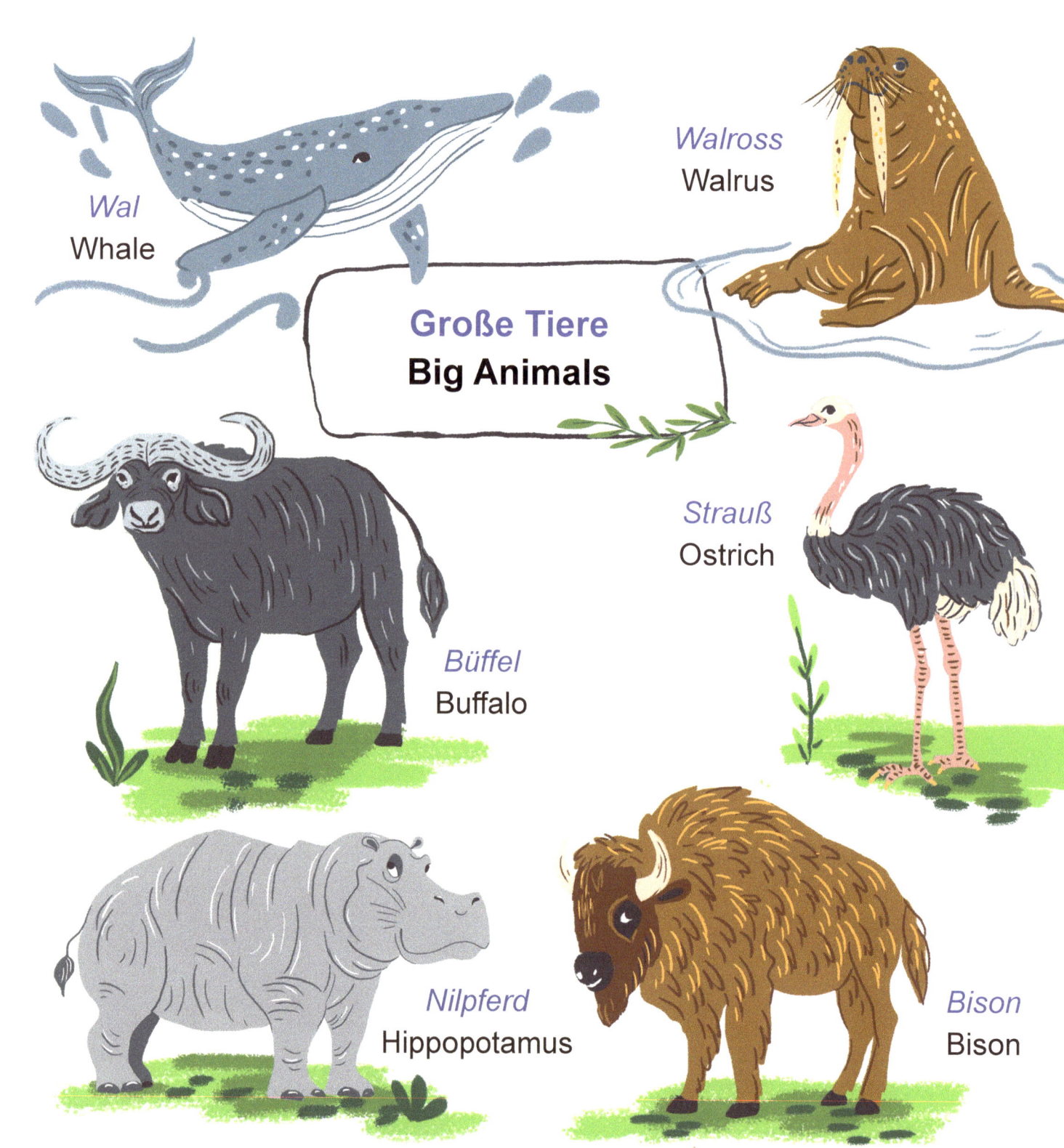

Kleine Tiere
Small Animals

Chamäleon
Chameleon

Spinne
Spider

✦ *Ein Strauß ist der größte Vogel, aber er kann nicht fliegen!*

✦ An ostrich is the biggest bird, but it cannot fly!

Biene
Bee

✦ *Eine Schnecke trägt ihr Haus auf dem Rücken und bewegt sich sehr langsam.*

✦ A snail carries its home on its back and moves very slowly.

Schnecke
Snail

Maus
Mouse

Ruhige Tiere
Quiet Animals

Marienkäfer
Ladybug

Schildkröte
Turtle

Fisch
Fish

✦ *Eine Schildkröte kann sowohl an Land als auch im Wasser leben.*
✦ A turtle can live both on land and in water.

Eidechse
Lizard

Eule
Owl

Fledermaus
Bat

✦ *Eine Eule jagt nachts und benutzt ihr Gehör, um Nahrung zu finden!*
✦ An owl hunts at night and uses its hearing to find food!

✦ *Ein Glühwürmchen leuchtet nachts, um andere Glühwürmchen zu finden*
✦ A firefly glows at night to find other fireflies.

Waschbär
Raccoon

Vogelspinne
Tarantula

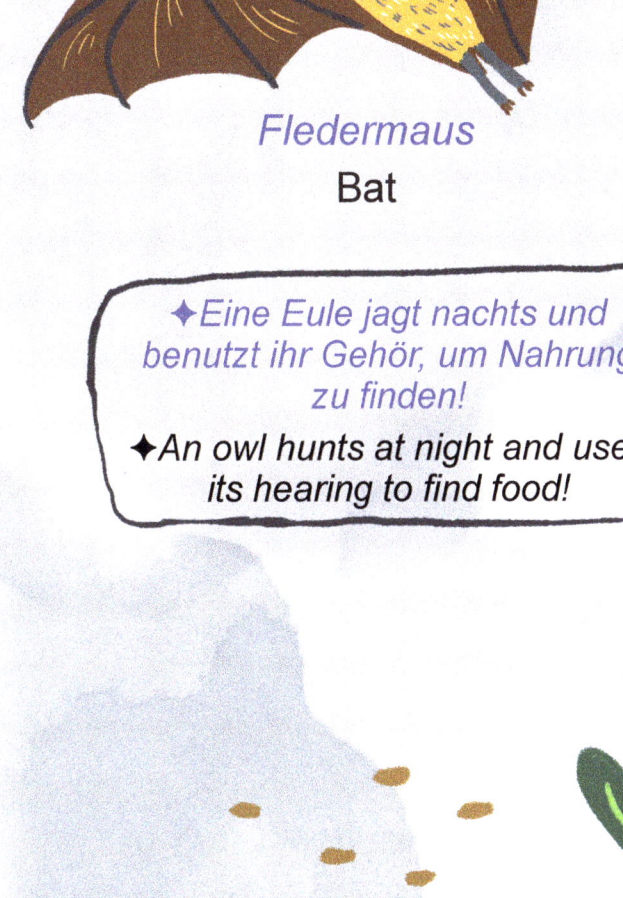

Bunte Tiere
Colorful Animals

Ein Flamingo ist rosa
A flamingo is pink

Eine Eule ist braun
An owl is brown

Ein Schwan ist weiß
A swan is white

Ein Oktopus ist lila
An octopus is purple

Ein Frosch ist grün
A frog is green

✦ *Ein Frosch ist grün, damit er sich zwischen den Blättern verstecken kann.*
✦ A frog is green, so it can hide among the leaves.

Tiere und ihre Jungen
Animals and Their Babies

Kuh und Kalb
Cow and Calf

Katze und Kätzchen
Cat and Kitten

✦Ein Küken spricht schon vor dem Schlüpfen mit seiner Mutter.

✦A chick talks to its mother even before it hatches.

Huhn und Küken
Chicken and Chick

Hund und Welpe
Dog and Puppy

Schmetterling und Raupe

Butterfly and Caterpillar

Schaf und Lamm

Sheep and Lamb

Pferd und Fohlen

Horse and Foal

Schwein und Ferkel

Pig and Piglet

Ziege und Zicklein

Goat and Kid

www.ingramcontent.com/pod-product-compliance
Lightning Source LLC
LaVergne TN
LVHW072004060526
838200LV00010B/275